POEMS: NEW AND SELECTED

POEMS

New and Selected

by Melville Cane

NEW YORK

HARCOURT, BRACE AND COMPANY

Typography by Robert Josephy
PRINTED IN THE UNITED STATES OF AMERICA

NOTE. This collection of 114 separate pieces includes 38 poems which have never before appeared in book form. The others, many of them revised, constitute that part of my earlier work which I wish to preserve. "January Garden" and "Behind Dark Spaces," the volumes in which they were first published, are now out of print. Four of the five sections into which the present book is divided contain the more serious poems; the fifth section is definitely lighter.

M. C.

Many of these poems have heretofore appeared in *The American Scholar*, *Books* (*The New York Herald Tribune*), *The Commonweal*, *The Conning Tower* (*New York World and Herald Tribune*), *Contempo*, *Contemporary Verse*, *The Dial*, *The Forge*, *The Guardian*, *Harper's Magazine*, *Larus*, *Life*, *The Menorah Journal*, *The Nation*, *The New English Weekly*, *The New Freeman*, *The New York Sun*, *The Saturday Review of Literature*, *Scribner's Magazine*, *The Sewanee Review*, *The Southwest Review*, *The Stage*, *The Virginia Quarterly Review*, *Voices*, *The Yale Review*. Some have likewise been reprinted in Untermeyer's *Modern American Poetry*, *The New Yorker Book of Verse*, and other anthologies.

CONTENTS

PART I: RECENT

TWO STARS

Two stars lie caught in a tree.

A shriveling angle
Of sight,—that snares a star in a tangle
Of leaves,—that shrinks a star to a spangle!

I have only to stand, to free them,
To step three steps, to see them
Clear of earth and true to sky,
Eye to eye.

Two stars rose from a tree.

DAWN HAS YET TO RIPPLE IN

What is this that I have heard?
Scurrying rat or stirring bird?
Scratching in the wall of sleep?
Twitching on the eaves of sleep?
I can hear it working close
Through a space along the house,
Through a space obscure and thin.
Night is swiftly running out,
Dawn has yet to ripple in,
Dawn has yet to clear the doubt,
Rat within or bird without.

ALL I KNEW

There was no reason, no warning;
All I knew—you were there!
As infallibly there
As the crystal air
That April morning.

There was no hint or suggestion
Of person or past;
I moved alone, serene in a vast
Non-human scheme, in a harmony cast
Too right for question.

I was one with the rising season,
With April's every leaf and earliest bud;
April's crystal flood
Sent a new fire streaming in the blood.
No warning, no reason!

EACH TO EACH

We were closed, each to each, yet dear.
We were taut with a covert pride;
We were tied
With a throttling fear;
We were undefined
And blind.

We were caught when we sought to reach;
We were mute when we strove for speech.
We were closed, each to each, yet dear.
We were vapid, polite, obscure
Through a merciless flood of pain;
We were trivial through strain;
We were desperate to endure.

Then a locked word slipped from your heart,
Like warm rain dropped on mine,
And the fog that had held us apart
Thinned,—we could dimly divine
The one we had groped for in vain.

And my hand touched yours, and the pain
That clutched and withered had fled,

And the fear and the pride lay dead,
And at last we were free, we were plain.

We were closed, each to each, yet dear.
We are close; we are clear.

IT DIGS A DOUBLE GRAVE

Your pain
Is a weight of stone
Upon my heart; your pain
Is mine.

Your pitiful eyes entreat,
Your lips beseech;
Our eyes, our lips, meet
In silent speech;
We are one,
Under your pain.

But love is less than love
That cannot give or save,
And when love closely cleaves
To that for which it grieves
It digs a double grave.

To part you from your pain,
To set you free,
I must myself be free
Or else be slain.
Loving, detached, still,

8

I must call on brain and will
Ever to cool and steel
This heart, too eager, lest it overfeel.
Then, only, can I heal.

EMILY DICKINSON

1830-1930

Enclosed within a hedge
Of privet, doubts and nays,
A burning spinster paced
Her clipped New England days.

While pretty singers droned
A local, nasal hymn,
She raised a timeless voice;
It reached the spatial rim.

She never saw a moor,
She never saw the sea,
Yet from a hilltop in her heart
She scanned Infinity.

CLARENCE DAY

(Died December 28, 1935)

The foe that crippled his frame,
That sought to stifle the flame,
Itself was trapped in the frame,
Singed by the flame,—
Stopped, surprised by a spirit
Which, having no call to fear it,
Counter-attacked, pursued
With weapons shrewd,—
Humor and fortitude.

A BODY RESTED ON A BED

A body rested on a bed,
Lacking breath;
Someone, leaning over, said:
"This is death."

Freed of passion, clear of storm
Was the face;
What had been a driven form
Wore grace.

Many mourners came to mourn
With "Alas"!
And with "Man of woman born,"
"Flesh is grass."

Many feeble tears they shed
For their friend,
As dispirited, they said:
"This, the end;"

And they stuffed a hollow thing
In a hole,—
Blind!—while a soul
Took wing.

I REMEMBER DISTINCTLY

I remember distinctly the time, when I said
To myself, as the thought,
Unsought,
Flashed through my head:
"Some day I shall see you no more;—
You will be dead."

I remember distinctly the place,
Where I said, face to face
With myself: "Some
Day it will come, it will come;
The dread summons will come."

And I said I must waste
No time,—there is not a moment to waste,
To school the heart for its burden,
To harden
The frail, irresolute will.

And I labored, I built, until
I fancied the imminent blow
As a scattering, impotent blow
Against a texture, toughened and tuned
To any threatened wound.

13

But out of the black
A thunder crack!
The will is riven,
The heart cloven.

THE TASK

How to cope
With the flight of hope;

Under despair
How to endure,
(Endure! Endure!)

And be more than a leaf
On the gale of grief,

And perceive, as only a fraction,
The pain and distraction.

How, in the perilous instant,
To hold, how dimly, the constant;

How dimly,
The way, the meaning, the mystery.

How, in the clutch of extinction,
Still to function, human!—

This is the task, the prayer,—that I may save
The suffering god within, that he may live,
And greatly live, beyond the grave.

PETITION

To be still
As a hill,
To be cool
As a pool,
To dare
To be bare,—
To be nil;

To surrender the will
That the will may be free
To submit, as the sand to the sea;

That the hope
May take shape,
As the sand from the sea;

That the dream,—
No longer a dream,—
Shall finally be;

That the soul
Shall be earthless,—
Earthless and whole.

RURAL DUMPHEAP

This rusty mound of cans,
This scatter of tires and pans,
This litter of mattresses and twisted springs,
This rotting refuse, these abandoned things
Malodorously flung,—this impudent pile
That dares to choke the current, to defile
The innocent season,—all are man's.

Man's inhumanity to sod
Makes countless snow-drops mourn,
And every gentle seed that's born
Gives battle for a dishonored god.

Within the heap, and darkly, heaves
The growing mutiny of leaves,
While down the valley bird to bird
Relays the rallying word,
And courage calls on every breeze
To armies of anemones,
And triumph scales the parapet,
A host of violet.

O man, where is thy victory?
Despite this blight of tins,
The fern persists and cleaves and wins,
And, gladly, spring begins.

NIGHT AT NOON

The early morning sparkle disappeared
With the blue; by noon the sun was blurred.
Lower, ever lower,
The sinister and leaden
Element extended, ever making duller
The meagre residue of color.
Nothing remained to deaden.
It seemed the end of day, of life,—the end.
Then as the final moment of despair
Let down a subtle weight upon the air,
Its ruthless pressure forced a feeble stir;
The stir persisted, struggled to defend
Its dubious motion, spread to the inner
Reaches of the dark. The pall grew thinner,
Reluctantly withdrew
Within itself. No hidden sun pressed through.
And yet, though imperceptible to sight,
One grew aware it was no longer night.

HYMN TO NIGHT

Now it grows dark.
Red goes
Out of the rose;
Out of the lawn
Green's withdrawn;
Each buttercup now yields
Its gold from blurring fields;
Larkspur and sky surrender
Blue wonder.

We were dark within, we relied
For our strength on the nourishing sun;
Now it is under and gone.
Now, as the light grows duller,
We, who had flourished on color,
Stand, in the ever-deepening shade,
Bereft, dismayed.

We were dark within, it was death
We saw, we had never seen
Within the dark, we had never known
The spark, the vital breath.
If only we had known
That black is neither loss nor lack

But holds the essential seed
Of mortal hope and need!

Now sheltering dusk,
Shepherd of color and light for dawns unending,
Tends the holy task.

Praise be to black, the benign,
No longer malign,
Prolonger of days!
Praise the preserver of shine,
The keeper of blaze!

Praise Night,
Forever praise
Savior Night,
Who surely stays
The arm of time,
Who guards the flame,
Who hoards the light.

Praised be the Night.

PRESENCE OF SNOW

So rare, so mere,
You cannot hear
It brush against the stillness or impair
With faintest stir
The poised, suspended air.

So rare, so mere,
And yet imponderably clear;
You cannot see, yet see
The secret flow
Of imminent snow,
Although
The softest breath has yet to free,
The gentlest current yet to take
The first bewildered flake.

APRIL FLURRY

This tardy April blast
Is winter's final thrust;
It cannot master
Or halt invincible spring,
But only bluster
And scatter and drive
Out of a cloudy hive
A swarm benign.

White bees,
Without hum, without sting,
Drift through boughs of pine.

Directionless they rove,
And unintentioned, these,—
Freed
Of any
Flowery greed,
Incurious of honey.

HITHER AND THITHER

The way of snow is hither and thither,
The restles way of to and fro,
Impatient of the fixed, the mean,
Too accurate law, the strict machine.

The way of snow is hither and thither,
The twisting way of criss and cross;
Needles ply, the fluent threads
Gather and join; the wonder spreads.

The way of snow is hither and thither,
The fitful way of slant and stray;
It spins a cloth of powdery spume,
Wind's the shuttle, sky the loom.

The way of snow is hither and thither,
The floating way of drift and lift.
Perceive
The flaky weave!
Divine
The white design!

FLASH!

Skip of chipmunk;
Spring of frog;
Swoop of hawk;
Strike
Of snake;
Leap of dog;
Dart of trout;
Cat-pounce!—

Flashes! born
Of body-scorn,
Dashing, dashing out,—
Unbound
To ounce
Or pound.

OUT OF CHAOS

Out of chaos One,
Sole, inchoate, unrelated.
Out of chaos One,
More than naught,
Less, alone, than One;
Not yet the first,
Yet the beginning.

Then, the follower, Two,
Creator of after,
Producer of time;
Two, the complement,
Author of space,
Fulfiller of One.

Now Two, the leader,
Shaper of plan,
Forerunner of faith,
Carrier of Three.
(Trinity
Holding infinity.)

RIVER-TOW

Now the tug,
Bellwether of a flock of sheeplike barges,
Stoutly, pluckily charges
The tricky current,
Nudges
Into single file the errant,
Stupid string, trudges
Up the river runway, under bridges
Massively retreating.
Now, beyond the bend, a muffled bleating.
Here, the widely heaving snake
That parted waters make.

ANCIENT ORGAN GRINDER

Her form a crook,
Her arm a crank,
An ageless witch
Forever stirs and brews the dregs of music.
"Sweet violets,
Sweeter than all the roses."
The metal rust has worn away the song.
The dismal ghost of song hovers and whines.
A coin drops flat in the empty cup.

PESTILENCE

"Has the planet begun to spin in the wrong direction? Is
the oxygen leaving the atmosphere?"

STUART CHASE.

Darkly
They swarm, they blacken the sky,
Egyptian plague descends upon the Rhineland;
It is The Swastikas.

Madly,
Careening as a clumsy tank revolves,
In sinister formation they bear down,
A locust-cloud
Of Swastikas.

Blindly,
Hungry with hate,
They seethe, overrun, lay waste,—
Nibble the leaf,
Nip the stalk,
Wither the bud,
Sap the root.

They clutch the hands of the clock,—
Back! they pull the hands back.
Seconds tick backwards,
Hours circle into yesterday.

They hear the command:
"Left foot forward!
Advance into the barbarous past!"

They crawl away from the sun,
Reversing time.

Now it is night.

ALL ARE ONE

Gently,
Evening enters the garden,
Gently the garden, every flower, responds.
Stretched full-length in the swing
I see the settling swallows, the silent birch,
The peaceful roof behind the birch,
The cross-bar of a distant pole beyond,
And, close before me on the darkening lawn,
You, deep in a steamer-chair,
Gently yielding to sleep.

Now, in this precious moment of perfect June,
You, I, swallows, birch, lawn,—
That love and fly and wear green leaves and die,—
The insensate roof, the dim, inanimate pole,
All are one.

PART II: LAND AND SEA
AND SKY AND SUN

ENGADINE

In the high hills,
In the hollows of the high Swiss hills,
Far above the lake that sleeps
So still, so far below,
Lies an airier pool.
Its springs arise in fragrant space
Above the wild flowers,
And not a stream that flows therein
Flows through earth.
Across uneven pastures,
By the shores of the high pool,
Lumbering cows munch bright colors,
Trample on fragrance.
From heavy throats of ever-hungry cows
Soft bells dangle.
Cows amble,
And sound runs and ripples from the bells,
Filling the pool.
Gay and sunny are the waters of sound.

In Alpine hills
A pool is fed by bells.

TOO DELEBLE, ALAS!

Now that the sun has passed
Beneath the west,
Now that the rosy spread
Begins to fade
And after-light is thinning,
Night advances, winning
Inch on golden inch.
Too deleble, alas!
The dapple on the branch,
The shimmer on the grass;
The yellow-green too frail
On apple-leaves that pale.
Violet dims, night hastens,
Blue lessens, black fastens;—
Not a thing the eye shapes
Escapes.

FRAIL LIGHT

When streets are mounds of frozen mud
And the blood
Beats slow,
And above the town
The sky sags damp and brown,
And the raw February ebb
Carries the threat of snow, more snow,—
Through the steaming opaque mass
Frail lemon light may pass
And pierce the thickest vapors
That shroud skyscrapers,
And make a warm aërial alley,
So that the mind may sniff
The most faint and fleeting whiff,—
Arbutus trailing across an awakening valley.

SNOW TOWARD EVENING

Suddenly the sky turned gray,
The day,
Which had been bitter and chill,
Grew soft and still.
Quietly
From some invisible blossoming tree
Millions of petals cool and white
Drifted and blew,
Lifted and flew,
Fell with the falling night.

THE STORM IS BROKEN

All day long the smash of the sea
Against the rocks;
All day long the gulls scream frantically,
And one crow mocks.
Out of the sea a hurricane
Has driven, hour on hour, with mounting tide,
The wild relentless rain
Across the countryside.
Somewhere in the obliterated west
A sun lies lost.
Evening birdlike hovers
Over wagon-ruts that now are little rivers.

The storm is breaking soon;
A tattered cloud
Meagerly veils the proud
Reluctant moon.
Motionless are leaf and fern.
Fireflies fantastically turn
On and off their green and yellow lights.

This is one of the clean and mellow nights
That follow rain in June.
Flurry of unseen wings;

An upland cowbell rings,
While, over the impenetrable marsh,
Bull-frogs harshly
Strum their stubborn strings.

I HAVE SEEN

I have seen:

A yellow butterfly
Steer for the harbor of a tiger-lily;

A snowy gull
Spin ascending spirals round a spruce;

A foolish June-bug
Sprint with a shooting star across the night.

And once
On a wild black road
I saw a summer moon
Weave a web of gold
Out of a humming stretch of telegraph wires.

SANDPIPER

Out of the dunes
Pipe! Pipe!
Hidden in silvery grasses
Pipe! Pipe!
Bodiless sound running along the slope—
Pipe! Pipe!
Playing itself—a small boy's nickel fife!
Magic!

Out of the sands
That swirl in smoky strands
The wind blows a shape,
Weaves a coat of feathers,
Twists a bit of wire into legs,
Breathes upon a whistle till it sings.

Wind,
Sidewalk vendor of toys,
Pulls a string—
The funny creature's scooting down the beach!
In and out,
In lines and curves,
In tangled loops and complicated esses,
It prints an inchwide track of clover leaves.

Wind presses a spring.
A flash!
The thing
Becomes a flying bird
That undulates in rhythm with the surf.
Then—splash!
It rides an instant on the shifting swell,
Rises again on shining wings,
Races into the horizon,
Wheels,
And swiftly follows tumbling breakers home.

Up from the water's edge
A fresh wet track of stenciled clover leaves.
Pipe! Pipe!

NORTHWINDS IN MAY

The lawn is warm with peace,
Trees shine with joy,
May is a violet song.

Now the world turns cold,
The trembling garden moans,
Panic clutches the bushes.

Northwinds, they seem to know,
Hate things that bloom and grow.

Mobs of lynching northwinds
Slash the leafy hedge,
Dismember the orchard,
Spill the blood of lilacs,
Deflower the spring.

FIREFLIES

Violet fades in the west,
Daisy-fields darken,
The country road is a road no more.
One star gleams;
Night stirs.

Wingèd sparks rise above the grasses,
Dart,
Swerve,
Circle,
Spiral
Underneath the lilac-hedge,
In and out of peonies,
Down among the hollyhocks,
Over by the rose-vine.

Winds blow,
Sparks fly,
Higher, higher,
Through the ancient maples,
Through the richest gloom of the tall New Eng-
      land maples,
Through the thick black foliage of my soul.

LAST NIGHT IT SNOWED

Dent! dent!
Hollow, blunt
Din of eager shovels, cracking
The warm husk of sleep, breaking
Open day.

Dent! dent!
Clipped chant
Of iron cuts
The knit air,
Chips a clear
Powdery way
In airy snow,
In earthy snow;
Hits
The case
Of ice at the base;
Splits
And severs, flesh from bone,
Ice from stone.

Dent! scrape!
Dent! scrape
Wintry dregs
From city flags.

FOG

1

MONSTER

Fog is a crawling monster.
Soundless, unseen,
With spidery stealth,
A thousand clammy tentacles
Surround, clutch, crush.

Fog is a sucking monster.
A thousand ravenous tongues
Lap the blue from the sky,
Lick the gold from the sun,
Swallow the sea,
Devour the land.

Land and sea and sky and sun
Now are one,
Slaty and dun;
One and none.

Horns moan terror.
Bells toll death.

2

MAGICIAN

Wrapped in a cloak
Of gray mystery,
Fog, the magician,
Steals tip-toe out of the sea.
In seven-league boots
He skims across the sky,
Blowing out the sun,
Blotting out the blue.
On cobweb wires he slides to earth,
Glides through gardens surreptitiously,
And sponges every color out of flowers.
Churches, houses, trees,
He wipes like chalky outlines from a slate.

Fog says: "Presto"!
And birds turn into nothing as they fly,
Men grow vague and vanish.
Fog lifts his hands!
And motor-cars roll off into a void,
Dogs evaporate,
Cats dissolve to bodiless meows.

Noiselessly, peacefully,
The old world ends.

46

Nothing remains
But fog and me
And another world to be.
Slowly, dimly,
I seem to feel
A little of the wonder and the joy
That must have gladdened God in the begin-
ning,
Creation before him.

3

WHITE

Gently
On myriad soundless wings
White fogs glide,
Alight,
A flock of doves
With breasts of down.

The sky was black
With rain
But now is soft
With feathers,

Burying the black world
Underneath the white.

Nothing can be seen;
Everything grows clear.

DEEP IN WAGON-RUTS

Deep in wagon-ruts
Blue frost settles.
Crystal lilies
With silver petals
Whiten blue pools.
Shadows
On stiffened meadows
Spread blue the snow.
A last quiver,—
The strangled river
Glazes ice-blue.

YELLOW BUTTERFLIES

In the baking dust of the country road,
Mid-summer noon,
A hundred lemon triangles
Each poised on a point,
No motion.
You step toward me,
The air fills with flying gold,
Yellow wings make yellow waves.

AEROPLANES IN JUNE

Over the garden hangs a sultry humming.
Through branches heavy with heat
Humming-birds dart hotly.
Above the barn, the elms, the glittering steeple,
Hungrily hums a swarm of cosmic bees.
Across that meadow of cloud they move,
And up that hill of shining sky
In fragrant airs of unseen flowers
They fly
Straight to the earthless honey of the sun.

ALTHOUGH OCTOBER GLOWS

Although October glows
It glows like the heart of an ember.
No need of black and shriveling December
To mark the close.
More radiant now than when the buds unfold,
The world consumes in gold
And death assumes the color of the rose.

AUGUST NOON

Cloud-bales hang,
Trees drowse
On heavy hills.
Cicadas tingle electric,
Flies make roving loops of sound,
Time lies bound in chains on the baking hay-
    pile,
Motion has fled the planet,
Carrying the breezes with her.

IN THE HARBOR

Like white butterflies
That skim meadows
And sip clover,
A fleet of fluttering sails
Wing the bay,
Sniffing salt.

JUNE RAINSTORM

Like a chicken-hawk,—
Savage plunge from the blue,—
June rain,
You strangle the peony stalk,
With a murderous wrench you strew
The lawn with pain.
Then off with your prey in the gale,
Downy petals spreading the tale.

ONE BY ONE

One by one,
Branch to branch,
Leaves topple,
Zigzag
Through motionless October,
Struggle,
Founder;—
Golden birds
With broken wings.

BATLIKE

A wheel of fire
Spins a red descent
Behind the western rim,
Trailing sparks.

Sparks, dustlike, settle.
Tracks fade in the sky
As the wake of a fish in the sea.

Rising,
Without a sound,
From high and undiscoverable nests,
Evening winds,
Batlike, start their flight.

THE NIGHT RIDES PAST

The night rides past;
The mad leaves whirl
Behind its flying wheels.
Odors chase like farmers' dogs
The night riding past,—
Grapy, cidery essences,
Raw, rank skunk,
Spicy hickory hearth-smoke,
Tar, trailing oil.
Sounds race with odors,
Lights race with sounds.
An owl whimpers by,
Headlights swoop,
A shocked fox barks.
The night rides past.

FROM A DECK CHAIR

Whenever the steamer dips
Within its careening ellipse
It leans on the slope of the sea,
The sliding hill of the sea.

Whenever the steamer lifts
The hillside flattens and shifts,
Descends, and drags a sail
Down with it under the rail.

FINE RAIN

Fine rain
Drills with steel
Through ice;

Strings silver berries
On black branches;

Weaves sky
With sod.

NOT EVEN

Not even a footstep
On the black frozen road,
Or the rustle
Of dead leaves,—
Not a leaf on the branch.

Not even the crackle
Of ice on the night,
Or the twitter
Of one bird
Before dawn.

Only a shutter
Flap—flap—flapping. . . .

SNOW IN APRIL

Sun is young in the year,
April is tender,
Pink tips appear
On branches slender.
Brown earth, stiff with cold,
Loosens green and gold.

Silver shine in the sky
Darkens to leaden;
Snarling winds fly,
Shrivel and deaden.
Snow-armies crush
Bough and bud and bush.

Venturous spring!
And, for what reason
This sorrowful thing—
Throttling a season?
Chilling in birds their song,
Choking the song?

Perilous birth!
Too early hour!
Detain, under earth,

Each delicate flower.
Winter must lengthen
Spring to strengthen!

Cover with white;
Green blades whiten.
On jonquil-gold spread winter-white;
The opening soil tighten.
Shelter, restrain the spring!
Till sky and sod and robins sing.

NOW, THROUGH THE AUTUMN
NIGHT

Now, through the autumn night,
Assertion of crickets,
Insistent, incessant, vain.
This is no music, no singing,
Only the desperate clinging
To, clutching at, summer.
It has rounded, ripened, vanished.
It is finished.

Now, through the autumn night,
Fire-flies—
Once they strewed their sparks
Through dark valleys of June,—
Themselves are strewn,
In the road, in the ruts,
With leaves and scattering nuts.

Drops of quicksilver, dulled;
Faint lights, chilled.
Lights feebly open, close,
Open, close,
Never again to rise.

Now, through the autumn night,
Defiance of crickets,
Shrill, dogged, futile.
In the dust, in the ruts,
Faint, feeble lights;—
Heart-beats!

Beating, now, is stilled.

PARIS IN A RAINY AUGUST

Sunless days,
Windless skies,
Ceaseless rain.
A heavy doom
Hangs over Paris in the sultry gloom.
On every street, in every park,
Plane-trees crackle, slip their bark.
Leaves shrivel,
Drift, dishevel
Dismal paths, their yellow rust
Powders in the common dust.
Paris, buoyant as a fountain,
Inexhaustible as a mountain-spring—there she
    lies,
Gasping, light fading from her eyes.
Fungus-mould
And green-damp
Spread smooth, iron-cold
Fingers round her throat,
Clamp
Her heart. Paris is dead;
A leaden layer of cloud
Will soon become her shroud.

Who will weep and who will gloat?
And who will keep
The vigil over her last and loneliest sleep?
Through the corrosive
Night, the explosive
Mockery of taxi-horns.
Who mourns?

Dull dawn of death!
And a breathless ravening choir
Of carrion sparrows twitching with desire.

PART III: I HAVE HEARD

I HAVE HEARD

I have heard
The arrested cadences of bells
When bells no longer sway;
I have found
The sound that swells from silence,
That dwells and drifts in silence following sound;
I have known
The melody
That dies in throats of birds.
And now, at last, I hear
The call you never voiced, I never answered;
Now you have ceased to call.

OLD FASHIONED SONG

You are to me a delicate flower
And life is flinty soil; with dread
I tremble that some cruel power
May tear you from your perilous bed.

I see your passionate beauty sway
Beneath the warring winds of love,
Now bent to earth, a piteous prey,
Now riding calm, the storm above.

May stars now baleful softly yield
Before your dear divinity,
May gods and men forever shield
Your sweet beseeching frailty.

OCTAGONS AND ROSES

Since I prefer octagonals to circles,
And since I crave the odor and color of roses,
May I, therefore, lop their curves,
Square their petals?
Roses have rights,
I, desire.
Should I mutilate the rose
I should violate desire.
One should seek elsewhere for octagonals.

DIFFERENCES IN TIME

Though it is dawn with you in Germany,
New York and I are still in heaviest night;
The sun prefers you in his circular flight,—
Six hours later I shall begin to see.
But were I there, you here in place of me,
And the unreversing sun revolved in quite
His usual ring, your miracle of sight
Would cancel space and my priority.

For you divine what lies behind the dark,
You find the caverns of eventual birth;
Like Noah's dove, above the tossing ark,
Your pinions steer toward unimagined earth;
Clairvoyantly you pierce the fog, and bright
Planets emerge. You are yourself the light.

ALONE, IMMUNE

She was not bound by mortal sight,
The stars were hers at noon.
Against the malady of night
She stood alone, immune.
The darkened fields of heaven
She ranged, and found the seven,—
Found and folded, one by one,
Seven colors lost with the sun.

BEHIND DARK SPACES

Somewhere, behind dark spaces,
Light races.
Pressure
Of rushing light
Tears a fissure
Across night,
A crack
In black less black.

Gradual starry withdrawal,
Cool of sky's vague pool,
Faint disclosure of rose,
Blue palely filtering through,
Under grim black, dim
Earth-green,—
Emerging scene.

Out of shreds, out of seeds, of utter grey,
Ultimate, brightly-woven, high-flowering day.

COUNTRY-HOUSE: MIDNIGHT

The key of the lamp clicks,
And as it locks the light,
The full black tide rolls in.

This had been a room,—
Warm wing-chair,
Peacocks strutting over chintz,
Blake's "Job,"
Telephone.

Black now floods the human spaces,
Drenches the hearth,
Topples every shape to shapelessness.

High, where a clock companionably sat,
A metal rat's-tooth
Evenly nicks and nibbles.

JANUARY GARDEN

Insidious, elemental cold
Foglike steals
Over garden-mold
And seals
The flower-border like a grave.

Lower, deeper,
Inch on inch,
It spreads its iron hold.

Pores through which the rain and sunlight flowed
Now, instead,
Are stopped with icy lead.

Take a sharp pick,
Break the harsh thick
Wintry metal:
Once you might have found
Springing through the ground
What goes to shape a petal.

Once from here did issue
Palpitating tissue
Of larkspur,

And the earthy mesh
Warmed the velvet flesh
Of pansies.

Once from here did stream
Odor, like a dream,—
That which, more than form or color, makes a
    rose a rose.

Beauty's womb
Is now a tomb
For frozen worms.

AN HOUR AGO

An hour ago the sky seemed permanent blue,
No sign could show
From what destructive roots these storm-winds
    grew,
Or why these black rains flow.

An hour ago the sea was gentle as death,—
What smouldering cause
Inflamed these foamy fangs, this poisonous
    breath,
These curving claws?

An hour ago my heart was shaken with pain;
I know not how
It came or ceased, or what may happen again
An hour from now.

FEELINGS

The cat killed a rat.
Magnificent in conquest
It lay basking.
How splendid the cat!
How horrid, how venomous the rat!
I breathed heavy with exultation
Over my enemy
Stiff and ugly in the dust.

It was no rat;
It was a baby rabbit,
Warmness running out.
Tender, curving back!
Soft, pathetic fur!
Innocent, wondering eyes!

The proud cat crumples and slinks,
Wind rips the roses,
A cloud bags the sun.

MANY RACES HAVE I RUN

Many races have I run
With fate and fate has always won.

Often less than by the inch
Of an intuition's flinch;

Often less than by the flash
Signalling: "Faith will crash!"

Often less than can be reckoned
By what
Is vaguely an inert spot
Within a second.

But most
I've lost
By the same mischance—
One back glance.

ON BARREN ROCKS I POURED MY BLOOD

On barren rocks I poured my blood
And, where I stood,
Before my clouded eyes
And under desolate skies
A miracle occurred.
Something stirred!
And over the changing planet
Flowers dared the peril
Of regions stark and sterile
And grasses pierced the granite.

THE MONTH IS MARCH

I had lain frozen
Through the long winter of terrible years.
Even pain
Gave no sign.
The ebb of life that lingered
Moved only as a torpor of the mind.
Then came a day—
Black as a day in a year barren of spring.
The heavens crashed, and crushed me; I was
    spent.
Yet, somehow,
Throughout the merciless beating of the storm
The miracle of your spirit pierced and mixed.

All that I know is this:
When, next day, I awoke,
The icy earth had cracked in a thousand cracks,
And seeds I had no memory of planting
Burst—
Like gaily colored crocuses
(White, blue, purple, gold!)—
Through to the sun
And flowered the world.

GRECO'S CHRIST IN THE LOUVRE

Nailed,
He has risen.

Among clouds
Weighted with ice,
Charged with storm,
Only a mortal shape suspends.

This cross,
A flag-pole planted on a mountain-peak,
This flesh
A flag.

SHE IS A SILVERY WATERFALL

She is a silvery waterfall,
A flying curve that grooves the cliff,
She is a pool of black and green,
A hundred feet below.

Long ago, a faltering stream
Dwindled,
Miles from the source.
Thinly to spread?
Sandily to expire?
Or dangerously to leap
Through space without a channel
And carve an earthless course?

She is a silvery waterfall.

PORTRAIT

Her face is a hard, dry mask,
Earth in early March.
Under and over something passes,
Spring wind in sunlit grasses.

A RAT

There's a rat in the wall,
A rat in the wall,
At the side of the bed,
Close to the head;
Gnawing a path
Through a thicket of lath,
Pawing a track
Through a forest of black.
Will it nibble and scratch
Till it loosens the latch
Of the portal of me?—
Will it scrape itself free?
Will it crumble and master
The wavering plaster
That leans between me and disaster?

UFFIZI

Tourists, personally conducted,
Behold you, Jesus,
Hanging,
Then pass on
To purchase picture postals
On the way to lunch.

TWO

Too heavy-footed
To fly,
He'll be rooted
To earth till he die.

Too airy, too light
To descend,
She'll spin out her flight
Till the end.

So tied,
So buoyed,
That neither
Can reach intermediate ether.

GOING TO MARKET

(Riverside Park)

The cattle-train jolted and halted;
Through slits in the dark
Trailed impotent cries of the dead—
Before they were dead.
I could see the whisk of a tail,
An ear or a nose pressed through;
I could smell the desperate warmth,—
But bodily motion and bodily breath
Were motion and breath of the dead,
And panicky bleatings of sheep
Were snarls and wails of the dead
Who knew they were dead.

Women and men who walked in the sun,
Children who played in the park,
Nurses and sailors, policemen and tramps
Stopped in their steps, trapped in their tracks,—
Caught in a spell by a shipment
Of sheep, who had guessed what the trip meant.

END OF DAYLIGHT-SAVING

When I was rich in April
They robbed me of an hour,
But, having many, many,
It was plucking one flower,
Or stealing one penny.

Brooks poured fast,
Flowers pushed thickly,
Hours slid past,—
All too quickly.

But brooks drain thin,
Flowers dry seedy,
Light draws in,
Now I'm needy.

The thief must have learned it,
And, giving no warning,
Mysteriously returned it
One crisp morning.

When I was rich in April
Before the early leaves,
Long before this ditty,
I never thought of thieves,
Or that thieves felt pity.

OUR APARTMENT IN AUGUST

The door-key turns;
I am caught in the coils of gloom.
Windows tighten,
Shades seal,
Shutters clamp,—
Knives that slit the dark in quivering halves,—
Forcing without this poisonous August night,
Squeezing within the airless black of the flat.
The only sounds
Crunch of a tar-ball rolling across bare floor,
Scratch of a mouse in terror behind the pipes,
Clocklike, hesitant drip in the kitchen sink.
A button pressed
And light bursts through a bulb
Exposing
Furniture shrouded,
Hangings bagged,
Tables bared,
Paintings swathed.

Why should my thoughts, beloved, turn to you?
This tomb holds no suggestion of your spirit.
You move in sunshine.
Your grace is like the sway of meadow-grasses

When summer breezes stir.
Your loveliness is like a mountain pool
That hears the melodies of birds at dawn.
Mine this vacant scene;
A flicker of life,
A scurry in dust
Through sunless halls.
I fling my windows open to the night;
The waters of the night fling me down.

ON A COMMUTER'S LAWN

Here stands what is left of a tree.
There was a time
When a trunk towered
And life flamed,
Roots to sky;
When youth raced
To the tips of delicate branches.
When the wind stirred
Green leaves stirred.
Under the sun
Fruit grew heavier,
Gathering color.

Tiger-growl of thunder,
Northwind, tiger-treacherous,
Tiger-lightning strikes to kill.

Three feet from the ground
A saw has made a smooth, flat cleavage,—
A clean stump, surgically satisfactory;
Perfect stand for a pot of geraniums.

ALONG ANY LOVELY ROAD

Once I was a hillside with a
Smooth, green cover.
Colors had their seasons;
Beauty followed beauty.
Over me commingled
Breath of living soil,
Spice of drying leaves,
Indian summer mist.
Then a man, practical,
Shrewd and cruel,
Tore me with a pick,
Gouged me with a shovel;
Found he had discovered
Sand and gravel.
Hoisted me in buckets,—
Buckets, buckets, buckets,—
I was a quarry and he
Quarried to the core.

No more flowers,
Birds fly past.
Now, instead of clover,
Dandelion and daisy,
Garbage is the poultice

That's spread upon the wound;
Now, instead of hare-bells,
Goldenrod and aster,
Refuse is the plaster
That's stretched across the wound.
Once I was a hillside
With a smooth green cover.
Colors had their seasons;
Beauty followed beauty.
Now, as the rains flow,
Now, as the years go,
Slowly the scar grows
Fainter,
Steadily fainter.

GULLS

Gulls, you are so absurd!
Only a moment ago,
Poised along that sandy, glistening bar,
You seemed to be settling down till the tide
    should cover.
Now
Bits of snow-white paper in a storm
Sprinkle Heaven with chaotic flight.
Why this silly hysteria,
That rips the sky with schoolgirl giggle and
    gabble?

Futile zigzags,
Broken spirals,
Drooping glide to soothing mud.
Refreshed, you rise and repeat,
You sink and repeat.

What is the right diagnosis
Of your ornithological neurosis?

I watch you whirl in white superb delirium
Against the deep-green density of pines.
Can it be

That you revolve in some mysterious rhythm
Beyond the earth-bound logic of my senses?
That your ecstatic unreason,
Your baffling disorderly beauty
An infinitesimal point may mark
On some wider arc?

And that your wild cacophonies
May sound a true harmonious phrase
In a music of infinite rapture
That I have yet to capture?

NIGHT IS BORN

Impalpably,
Night, the subtle fluid,
Drifts from the dome,
Streams from the soil,
Rings all horizons,
Penetrates, permeates, pervades.

Indistinguishable lie
Black sea, black sky;
Undimensional the land
And my outstretched hand.

OCTOBER NIGHT—WESTPORT

Out of doors a million gentle stars;
Winds of evening, strokes of tenderness;
Thud of fruit, dropping late.
Within the house
A quiet light in the lamp.
Strained boards relax.
Behind the plaster
Criss-cross mouse-play.
In the wing-chair shelter
You and a book,
Hand reaching toward the settle,—
Slices of apple, slivers of nut, cider-jug.
On the rug,
Swelling, falling, swelling, falling,
Warm mass of drowsing cat.
On the mantel
Tick-tock, tick-tock.
Logs burn thin,
Sag to embers,
Settling orange embers.

ONCE, AT TARASCON

Once, at Tarascon,
I saw a flock of sheep
Filling an ancient lane.
Sunset dyed their fleece with mauve.
Startled,
They bunched and huddled,
And panic ran along their backs
Like quicksilver.

LYING IN GRASS

August . . .
In high, dry grass.
Arm crooked,
Head cupped,
Ear sunk,
Flank pressed
Into earth.
Eyes are
Two field-mice,
Scurrying, scurrying
Through grass-tips,
Sniffing shadows,
Nibbling sun-glints,
Darting back
Into sleep holes.

THROUGH A BEDROOM WINDOW

From where I lie
The sky
Is twelve blue rectangles.
High in the topmost right-hand space
A dry leaf dangles
From a frozen bough.
Now,
Out of the upper air,
Clouds press from square to square
And pass without a trace.
Huddled on a perch of wire
That cuts in two the church's arrowy spire
A mute sparrow hoards its feeble fire.

 . . . .

Now there is only black, no shapes, no bars;
Nothingness, and cold emerging stars.

WINTER NIGHT

Winter-cold is the night.
Chiseled in deepest blue,
Each star-shape silver-white
Shines cold-clear down the sky's long avenue.
The rich moon with its broadly streaming flood
Washes with light
The earth whereon I stand.
The icy ether fires my smoldering blood,
The stars I breathe and feel,
The magic heavens my trembling senses steal,
Until, exquisitely unmanned,
My spirits swoon
With the delicious cold, the dark, the riding
    moon.

AT CHARTRES

Candles waiting to be lighted,
Cool bed of lilies
Set in the shade of arches.
Now, touched by flame,
Burning down to death,
Each bears its flower of gold.

CLOUDS

There were no flowers in the sky,
Only a cobalt field
Of glittering July.
Under
My gaze of wonder
You grew
From gathered dew,
Your soil the fertile breeze,
Your seed the hum of bees,
Rootless,
Stemless,
Earthless
Blossoms alone and complete.

Now though you retreat and disappear
Out of the singing sphere,
There shall be no lament for fleeting beauty,
No sighing breath
For this which is not death.
Rank decay or rot of leaf
Does not mar your passage brief.
Heaven bore you without pain,
Heaven a garden will remain,
Fragrant and without a stain.

DEATH

It is sweet, toward the end of day,
To step, out of the roar,
Out of the glare,
Into the room, it is still,
Into the flooding final light;
Sweet, as the noises fade,
As the pressure lifts,
To be wrapped in the warmth of the sun,
To be lowered gently in sleep.

Bruised but intact,
Sound in retreat,
I have slipped from the pitiless city
To the peace of the room,
The harbor of light,
The shelter of sleep.

Clear of pursuit,
Weary of flight,
I have fallen asleep in the ebbing sun;
Deeply,
With even breath,
I have sunk in the sea of the dark,—

Like a child, I have lain on the breast of the
    dark,
To awake,
To arise,
In a world of stars.

PART IV: LONGER

HOUDINI

The papers said:
"Houdini Dead!"
Racing newsboys yelled:
"Houdini dead! Houdini dead!"
People read, smiled:
"Just another front
Page publicity stunt."
But Houdini was dead.

How can one get away with it,—
The box-trick,—
How can one fool Death?

No one could fix the committee,
An undertaker, chairman.
Dead men play no tricks,
But was he "playing dead"?
How could a dead magician
Put it over a live mortician?

They clamped him with manacles,
Shackled his ankles,

Clapped him in a case,
Strapped him to his place,
Locked the lid.
He did what he was bid.
They kept the watch by day,
They vigiled him by night
In the sputtering candle-light.
He never left their sight.

They bore him from the house,
They caged him in a hearse,
(The hearse was framed in glass,
Was screwed with screws of brass,
And only light could pass).

They took him for a ride,
Captive, chained and tied;
They set him on the ground,
Coffined, fettered, bound,—
The damp November ground.
He made no sound.

The grave was dark and deep,
The walls were high and steep;
They lifted him and lowered him,
They shoveled earth, a heavy heap—

A rising heap, a dwindling hole.
A rabbi made a prayer for his soul.

II

Years ago, a mid-summer day,
Saugatuck, Long Island Sound.
Suddenly he stepped out on the shore,
Dropped his robe,
A bather,
Smiling, bowing, in the sun.
Incredulous ones
Peered within a packing case,
Felt for secret panels,
Tapped each side.
Strangers tied him, hand and foot and torse,
Hammered fast the top with nails of steel,
Roped and double-roped and tugged the knots.
A high derrick dipped,
An iron hook slipped,
Clinched the rope,
Pulled its dangling burden clear of land,
Plunged it in the waves.
Then, as it rose again, a swinging minute,
A swimmer stroked his triumph toward the bank.
To do the box-trick in water,
When the July sun is shining,

115

Is hard;
But, harder still,
On a cold November day
To swim through clay.

III

This was no mountebank,
No spangled juggler
Of rubber-balls and billiard cues and lamps—
This was and is and ever will be spirit.
There is a legerdemain
Unsensed by mortal fingers,
A clairvoyance
The perishable brain
Is hopeless to attain.
There is a heart-beat of the spirit;
No one can time it.
There is a blood, a muscle, of the soul.
Lithe is the spirit and nimble
To loose the cords of the body;
Wiry and supple the soul
To slip the strait-jacket of the flesh.

IV

Out of an unbroken grave,
Above unheeding mourners,

Before the sightless eyes of conjurors,
Houdini rose
And lightly sprinted down an aisle of air
Amid the relieved and welcoming applause
Of those already there.

SHAPELESS RAIN

I

What is this blight
That has bitten
And made brown
The uncorrupted bright
Blue above the town?
That has eaten
Away the sun,
Withering noon to night?

It is the slow corrosion of shapeless rain.
What barrier can resist
Pressure of mist?
Street by street it softly conquers,
Holds with chainless anchors.
The town surrenders to suspended rain.
Along the avenue, from sentry towers,
As dark more darkly lowers,
They are hanging
Rubies, stringing
Emeralds on the rain.
Eyes of creeping motor cars
Are sweeping golden stars,
Searching the dense, unfallen rain.

Dust whirls.
A gust takes a girl's
Scarf. Buses emerge,
Stagger, charge.
Confusion
Of scuttling feet. Collision!
A shower of weightless pebbles
Flung wet in the face,—
A trace
Printed on asphalt, spattering cobbles.

Ripe for escape,
The pent mixture
Slips into motion and shape.
The uncertain
Pervasive curtain
Wavers,—a texture
Of watery seams,
Of wiry streams.
Deftly, bit by bit,
Windy knives rip, slit.
Swift
With life teems the amorphous drift.

III

Silver rain is steadily drilling down.
Rain released releases the captive town.
Now the town is dancing to rhythmic rain,
Singing to lyric rain.

WE ARE AS FIREFLIES

Ever since the dawn,
A shower of gold, drawn
From a cloud of gold, has finely fallen,
Quiet as pollen.
Each minute particle
Affirms the shining principle—
Day!
Hovering like a skein
Of arrested rain,
Shy light
Swiftly diminishes,
Twilight
Vanishes.
Into earth, and under, run
The last dry rills of the sun.

Ever since the dawn,
Low in the bushes, deep in the lawn,
Innocent of nightfall
They have lived in perpetual lightfall.
Now they are black with fear
At death so cold, so near—
A frenzied swarm of utter
Confusion and flutter,

A seething ferment
Of animalcular torment.

Spent and numb with despair,
They drop (like withered berries
The wind shakes and carries)
Into the spreading pall.
They fall,
But all is not over; they stir,
Weakly extend, struggle to crawl.

They grope, they scurry
With a new fury;
They thread, they explore
The shaded floor;
They drill each secret pore.
They channel,
They tunnel,
They mine the fluid ore.

Rising above the grasses
A flurry of wings passes
Over gardens, under spheres;
This is the song one hears:
"Far in the ground
Lost is found!

Up from the dark
A rescued spark!
Out of the grave
We will save
A kernel
Of eternal
Light. We will fly,
Swinging grains of light.
Sowing the fruitful sky,
We will put an end to night."

TREE IN DECEMBER

Frost has sealed
The still December field.
Over fern and furrow,
Over the quickening
Within each meadowy acre,
Frost, invisibly thorough,
Spreads its thickening
Stiffening lacquer.

Above the field, beneath a sky
Heavy with snow stirring to fly,
A tree stands alone,
Bare of fruit, leaves gone,
Bleak as stone.

Once, on a similar glazed
Field, on a similar tree,
Dead as the eye could see,
The first man, dazed
In the first December, grimly gazed,
Never having seen
The miracle of recurring green,
The shining spectacle of rebirth
Rising out of frozen earth.

Snow fell and all about
Covered earth, and him with doubt.
More chill grew the air
And his mute despair.

Leaves that April had uncurled
Now were blown dust in the world,
Apples mellowing sweet and sound
Now were icy rot in the ground;
Roses August sunned in bloom
Now were less than lost perfume.

Had he seen the final hour
Of fruit and leaf and flower?
Had the last bird taken wing,
Nevermore to sing?
Never to fly in the light of another spring?

The man trembled with cold, with dread,
Thinking of all things dead
And his own earthen bed.

Trembling, he grew aware
Of a new quiet in the air;
Snow had ceased;
A ray came faintly through;
The wavering slit of blue
Vaguely increased.

Trembling, the first man gazed
At the glazed
And glittering tree,
Dead as the eye could see.

Whence came the sight
To read the sign aright?
The hint,—
The glad intimation, flashing:
"Wintry rains
Are blood in the veins;
Under snows and binding sleets
Locked roots live, a heart still beats"?

From what impalpable breath
Issued the faith,
The inner cry: "This is not death"?

PART V: LIGHTER

IN ZURICH

In Zurich,
Au *lac*,
As soon as it is June,
They deck the tables on the terraces
With yellow irises,
And serve a brand of scrupulously fine
Gay sunshine,
To mix with equally clear and sunny
Amber honey
And butter-balls, like curled tea-roses.
Then, if you so incline,
A draught, or two, or three, of wine;
And, as the blood begins
To sing with the violins,
One muses
And drowses.

ON SHABBY GREEN

In early April
On shabby green
Nervous robins pivot, balance,
Curve, dash, curve, dash,
Bill up, tail down,
Bill down, tail up.

Into shabby green
Thrusting robins peck!
Out of shabby green
Tugging robins pluck
Little lively things,
Things that dart and wriggle.

Fat and sated robins
Saunter and meander,
Loiter as they wander
Under bursting maples,
Over rugs of ruddy buds
Blown on shabby green.

BEGINNING TO RAIN

It seemed the first sharp spatter of rain
But only sound dripped from the branches.
Yet I'm not sure—
It may have been a warning of undropped drops,
Sent ahead
To get the leaves used to it.

CASUALLY

I was lying on the grass,
Thinking of nothing in particular,
When a maple-leaf settled beside me
And laughed in the friendliest fashion.
You have no idea
What a pleasant hour we spent together.

CONNECTICUT SUNDAY

January rain drips from wire and branch,
Drizzles glumly through the Connecticut Sun-
    day.
The cracked bell of the Catholic Church
Trails across the fog inertly,
Tolls flatly.
Listlessly the bell of the Episcopalians
Swings a limp reply.

COWS

Cows have such a serious look,
They must be thinking.
But I don't know—
I've seen
The same look
On men.

GUARDIANS

God in his infinite wisdom does not teach
The budding clover to respect its elders,
The incipient mountain-brook to be unselfish,
The sapling birch to love and honor its parents,
The April crescent to be polite to the stars,
The young spring rain to be careful where it
    spatters.
God never mentions duty to the hillocks,
Or ever says "Don't!" or "Stop!" to infant rain-
    bows,
Or preaches self-control to little lightnings
Or orderliness to adolescent thunders.

THESE AUGUST NIGHTS

I wish that the Metropolitan Tower
Were not as stiff as a church;
I wish it would bend, like a giant birch,
And birds would chime each quarter-hour,
And windows, ablaze with electric lights,
Would branch into leaf, these August nights,
And ripple the air
Over Madison Square,
And tenderly cover
Lover and lover.
But it won't even lean, it won't even lurch.
It's as stiff as a church.

NEWS

This blue-frost day
A feather
Lost in shining weather,
Floats through a cloud,
Slips down a chimney.

The papers refuse
To report the news.
They'd sooner say
(And tuck it away):
"11:05 A.M.,
Moon sets."

LADY-POET (OF EITHER SEX)

She loves to whittle
And shave her feelings
And save the peelings
Pretty and brittle;

Enjoys the titil-
lation and subtle
Play of verbal
Shuttle and burble;

Toys with mystic
Rapture and terror—
All in a narcissistic
Mirror.

IMPECCABLE

Each line ran fleet and flawless,
In perfect pairs, each rhyme;
No vocable, no syllable
But served the general chime.

Each adjective was fitting,
Each fitted noun correct,
Each metaphor and simile
Enriched the proud effect.

One sought in vain the tasteless,
Inept or crude or wrong,
One could not find the slightest lack
Of art, detect the faintest crack
To extricate the song.

ENCOUNTER

I roamed at twilight through a wood,
I saw that dusk would come anon,
When, high above me where I stood,
I met a weird phenomenon.

A gloomy screech upon a limb,
I could not trace it, beast or bird,
I could not see it in the dim
And deepening shade, I only heard.

"O furry shape, O feathery thing,
Malign, benign, whatever you be,
Reveal yourself!" A muffled spring!
It wabbled and confronted me.

It settled with an awkward tilt,
It listed badly to one side,
By nature most unkindly built,
The creature then replied:

"I am the Propaganda Bird,
Of right wing quite bereft,
From which it clearly is inferred
That what is left is left.

"I cultivate my special slant,—
You may esteem it lack of poise,—
And when I sing, the ignorant
Mistake the effect for noise.

"The bourgeoisie still dote on larks,
To them I'm just a bawling boss-cow,
They miss the melody in Marx,
The lyric tune that's pitched in Moscow.

"All themes of simple love and hate
Are ivory-towerish and arty,
Except when they articulate
Some vital tenet of our party.

"On wit and laughter down we clamp,
You must be solemn as the tomb, or
You win no welcome to our camp;
We've ostracized the sense of humor.

"Whate'er you write or sculp or paint
Is all as false as Ananias,
And worthless,—since it bears the taint
And blight of capitalistic bias.

"I practise proletarian art,
A preachment lodged in every passage,
I do my individual part
Announcing the collective message,

"Proclaiming love from man to man,
Maintaining all of us are brothers;
Our dogma's somewhat partisan,
We bar the point of view of others."

With this it ceased. The next I knew
I heard afar a something raucous,
Reminding me, as off it flew,
Of angry comrades at a caucus.

A dismal croak, a distant guggle
Assailed my unenlightened ear;
I thought I caught the words "Class Struggle,"
And then I still could thinly hear:

"I am the Propaganda Bird,
Of right wing quite bereft,
From which it clearly is inferred
That what is left is left."

ASKEW, WE ASK YOU

Gertrude—there's a good old scout!
What's it what's it all about?
Hear a tortured hemisphere
Begging you to make it clear.
Drop a clue or slip a hint
Touching on the what-you-print,
What-you-print and what-there's-in't.

Abdicate the role of sibyl,
At your secret let us nibble.
Pray divulge, reveal, disclose
In communicable prose
Why a rose a rose a rose.

Are you willfully obscure?
Are you puerile or mature?
We are anything but sure.

Are you spoofing or profound?
Is there sense within the sound?
Will you properly expound?

Is your highly Orphic text
Meant for this world or the next?
We concede we are perplexed.

Is it genius, is it sham?
Parlor game or cryptogram?
Will you answer kindly, Ma'am?

Are you hollow or a mine?
One remembers Shakespeare's line:
"Sermons lie concealed in Stein."

Gertrude answers, slightly bored:
"Gertrude is her own reward."

FOUNTAINS OF ROME

Throughout the starry Roman night
And through the shining day,
The fountains fling their crystal loops,
Or flash their diamond spray.
They're beautiful when hard at work
And likewise when they play.

LINES AFTER A MOTOR TRIP
THROUGH THE SOUTH

George Washington,
Parens Patriae;
Robert E. Lee,
"That my men may retain their horses";
Patrick Henry,
"Or give me death";
Thomas Jefferson,
"When, in the course of";
Stonewall Jackson,
"Dies like a dog";—
March on, march on!
Your shining names with us shall ever dwell,
Fixed to a first- or possibly second-
Rate hotel.

ORCHESTRA NOTES

Pity the wretched harp-player!
Lord, he must suffer a pang or two,
Sitting up there
For the whole of a symphony,
Plucking no more than a twang or two.

Pity the hapless drummer!
What man's lot could be glummer?
Tense with concern,
Waiting his turn
To release his appropriate bang or two.

And the scrupulous wielder of cymbals,
On pins and needles and thimbles!
Marking each beat
For the moment discreet
To crash his climacteric zing or two.
(He surely could tell us a thing or two.)

But what, if anyone misses?
Who gets the hisses, the odium?
Would anyone choose
To step into the shoes
Of the guy on the brink of the podium?

OPERATIC NOTE

Apparently the Nibelungs
Were never cursed with feeble lungs.

LITERARY NOTE

Walter Savage Landor
Never used and/or.

FORD SUNDAY-HOUR NOTE

After the glory, the ecstasy
Of "Götterdämmerung,"
Why should there always be,
Always be
W. J. Cämmerung?

WHITE HOUSE SONG

If only Justice Sutherland
Would migrate to some other land;

If, haply, Justice VanDevanter
Resigned instanter;

If James McReynolds' comprehension
Grasped the virtues of a pension;

If, fourthly, Mr. Justice Butler
Chanced to be the least mite subtler,
And took the hint that he is not a
Complete persona grata:

I'd say: "How now?" to Roberts,
I'd say: "Oh, yeah?" to Hughes,
And then I'd up and pick and pack,—
My Friends: I'd never lose.

THE WORLD AROUND US

Folks in Fordham
Die of bordham.

In Canajoharie
They just won't marie.

But in Yonkers
Love conkers.

These nights, at Cazenovia,
You sleep with blankets ovia.

Some move to Oneonta,
Others don't wonta.

Throughout the whole of China
There's not an Elk or Shrina.

And, likewise, in Canarsie,
One seldom meets a Parsee.

It's blackberry time at Pelham.
They can 'em, stew 'em, jelham.

A nudist fan at Hudson
Was warned to put his dudson.

A physicist at Chatham
Last Monday split an atham.

COME MARCH FIFTEENTH

Tempus is fugiting, deadline is beckoning,
Morgenthau's fidgeting, Morgenthau's reckoning.
Why is the brain, when it needs to coordinate,
Hopelessly negative, blank, insubordinate?
Why am I paralyzed, worse than a nincom-
Poop, when I'm threatened to figure my income?
Stomach's gone back on me, nerves are atingle,—
Why can't I tell if I'm married or single?
Why must I ask of my nurse or attendant
Whether I'm childless or own a dependent?

Profit or loss on the sale of securities,—
This is but one of the minor obscurities,—
Bonds in default at their wretched maturities,
Stocks that were sound but developed impurities.
How to apply all the proper percentages,
How to employ all the legal advantages,
How to deduct every possible charity,
What can be done with that debt of O'Flaherty?

Lucky the fellow who's on relief,
He gets his pay and he's spared the grief.
Why have I labored? What has it all meant,
When I must borrow to meet the instalment?

I'm muddled
And puzzled,
I'm puddled
And muzzled,
I'm worried
And harried,
And still can't tell if I'm single or married.

I can't subtract and I can't divide.
My troubles have added and multiplied.
The missus begs me to figure *her* tax!
Now, must a female submit to a sir-tax?
I just can't cope, I can't attack it,
I don't know one from the other bracket.
To be quite frank, it wouldn't hurt if I'd
Seek an accountant, duly certified.

For—
My spine needs starching,
And the Ides are Marching.

GILBERT AND SULLIVAN

England, O England!
We freemen owe thee much; in truth thou art a
Tyrant's scourge that dates from Magna Carta.
We thank thee, Britain, we don't mind con-
    fessing,
For many another truly unmixed blessing.

And, 'twere nothing short of hateful,
Yes, contemptible and petty,
Were we not supremely grateful,
Far beyond all other boons,
For Sir William's gay libretti
And Sir Arthur's golden tunes.

Pound the drum and sound the tuba,
Usher in the haughty Pooh-Bah;
Clash the cymbals, crash the chords,
For the dashing House of Lords,
(And for General Stanley's wards.)

Welcome, sweetly as you can, the
Sadly fated Iolanthe;
Listen to that witty thing
Brightly sung by Pitti-Sing,—
Blithe as blooming flowers in Spring.

Greet the gallant gondolieri,
Hail each semi-mortal fairy,
Pity, O! the hapless nurse,
Who, by carelessness or worse,
Infant charges did reverse.

Spurn the aesthete, sham and childish,
In a setting Oscar Wildeish,
Warbling: "Every rose has one thorn,
Every rose at least has one thorn,"
Or some master-piece by Bunthorne.

See the spurious and pompous
Blown to parts beyond the compass.
By the subtle stab of satire
Pose is pricked,—the merest flat tire,—
By the point of Gilbert's satire.

For Sir Arthur, greenest laurels,
For his carols and his chorals,
For his facile melometrics
Matching Gilbert's nimble pet tricks,—
(Patter-songs brings out their pet tricks.)

Here's every kind of fantasy
For any maid or man to see,

All proper for your aunt to see,
Who winces when she's shocked.
And here's a cornucopia
Of lenses from Utopia,
Corrective of myopia
Just dying to be mocked.

Here's a heaven to believe in
With an equitable god,
Who provides a perfect even
For each corresponding odd;
Where His Reasonable Highness,
Quite without the slightest fuss,
Mates each uncompleted minus
With a satisfying plus.
(Nothing's really so divine as
When a minus joins a plus.)

Hurray! for the shepherds and sailors,
The coolies and jailors.
Heigh ho! for the various series
Of bobbies and yeomen and peris,
The sisters and cousins and aunts,
The sinister coast of Penzance.
Ah me! for the maidens in vapory
Mystical Burne-Jones drapery.

Huzzah! for the heavy dragoons
And the Venice lagoons.

And so, bless
The jeu d'esprit, the rare noblesse
Of G. and S.

Now the final curtain falls,
While, responsive to our calls,
Still they caper and coyly dart,
All in the mode of D'Oyly Carte.

A la mode and à la Carte,
Savoy fare served à la Carte.

MOSAIC

Who, in the conduct of official duty,
Covers our unkempt Empire State with beauty?
Who is it voters, mindful not of party,
Acclaim with plaudits merited and hearty?
Who, the depression unending
Notwithstanding,
Biblically doubles each grassy blade,
Renews the green, augments the shade,
Making our pathway truly one of roses?
Obviously, Bob Moses.

The unemployed get work
To aid in his pet work
Of weaving a network
Of new ways
And through ways.
Each village and county,
Including Oswego,
Schoharie, Otsego,
Is blessed with his bounty.

For mister and madam
He spreads the macadam,
He smooths and massages,—

They fly past garages
And hamlets and churches
And hemlocks and birches,
And, as they alight to pour gas in their tanks,
And smear on the mustard and gobble the franks,
They pause to give thanks.

(Gather up the orange-peels,
Gather up the egg-shells,
Pick up all the papers
And stick 'em in the can!)

He cares for the lambs
And the ewes and the rams,
The gnus and the yaks and the camels,
And the higher assortment of mammals,—
The Swedes and the Poles and the Cabots,
The Murphys, the Cohns and the Babbitts.
Each creature of the jungle, O!
Enjoys its private bungalow,—
An air-conditioned, kitchenetted bungalow.

The cricket, bee and humble ant
Combine in one delirious chant,
And, as the bright day closes,
The bird who in the waning light

Was wont to call: "Bob White! Bob White!"
Now cries instead: "Bob Moses!"

(Dancing on the Mall,
Jazz for one and all,
We'll trip the light fantastic
In the moonlight on the Mall!)

All dingy and dark ways
He turns into parkways,
The swampy and grey ground
Soon blossoms as playground;
The withering landscape he sprinkles
And coaxes to life till it twinkles.
He renders first-aid with his tonics
To shrubs when they wilt in the Bronix.
He dredges the inlets
For froglets and finlets,
He opens the outlets
For traveling troutlets,
For Moses is king of the ooze,—
He is,—the magical king of the ooze.
He cleanses the dune and develops the beach
As far as his wide jurisdiction will reach,
And, finally, banishes squatters—
And yachters.

(Jones Beach is broad and clean,
Broad and clean, broad and clean,
Jones Beach is broad and clean,
My tan lady.)

He neither sleeps nor loafs nor dozes,
But digs and plants and sprays and hoses.
He leads us with unfaltering hand
Straight down into the Promised Land,
And is it grand? boy, is it grand?
And is it hard to understand
Why anyone composes
A psalm in praise of Moses?